Acknowledgements

For support and encouragement ...

Rob's mum (for seeing the possibilities, if not the reason), Rob's dad (for passing on the inherited interest for this work), Ed's wife, Agi (for infinite patience, and for eventually believing in the project), Ed's mum, Fereshteh (for boundless support and the suggestion that we 'try to do the book well'), Ed's dad, John (for inspiring a passion for language and freedom of expression), Rob's brothers, Alex (for wise advice) and Daniel (for Shitterton), Ed's brother, George (for his encouragement), Ozge (for constant support and understanding), Kerry (for Bottoms Fold and warm support), Sacha (for characteristically positive encouragement), Mike and Alison Esau (for a variety of suggestions and patiently waiting in the car), Ellie and Naps (for advice and direction), Clare and Rob (as trusted reviewers), and Satish (for international encouragement).

Thanks also to ...

Natalie Jerome (for the opportunity and guidance), Elizabeth Haylett at the Society of Authors (for patient, valued advice), Susan Smith (for encouragement), Mike Jones (for his Scratchy Bottom), Ian Bowskill (for help with Pant), Paul and Colin (for tolerating interruptions during a 1,100-mile cycle ride), David Cox (for suggesting Menlove Avenue), Positive Images in Richmond (for professional imaging), Sally Blouet (for excellent design advice) and all those who unwittingly suggested names or helped us along the way.

And while we're at it ...

Rob would like to thank Ed for his enthusiasm, challenges, pedantry, great friendship, and for choosing to join him on this journey. Ed would like to express immense thanks to Rob for inviting him to share this mammoth project – clearly Rob's generosity is surpassed only by his good judgement.

And finally ...

To the retired vicar who admired Back Passage with Ed, the man who ejected us from Shepherd's Bush station and all the passers-by who raised an eyebrow at us.

CONTENTS

THE TOP TEN

10|10|05

Explanation of the ranking system
The names presented in this book are ranked according to popular perceptions of rudeness. This was determined in an empirical manner, involving data-gathering from focus group participants. The results were carefully analysed to provide a rank order. This was then adjusted in line with the authors' expert judgement.

Authors' note
We would like to appeal to readers of this book to treat these places with respect; please accord privacy and peace to the people who live in these locations.

INTRODUCTION

B ritain has a history common to many islands: it is one of repeated invasion, occupation and assimilation. Each phase of this history has left its mark on our culture, architecture, language and place names. A rich mixture of Celtic, Norse, Anglo-Saxon, French and Latin has made the English language a gift to poets and writers. However, the nuances and double meanings so favoured by creative writers have also caused great confusion.

In this historical, exhaustively researched work, we present a number of place and street names which, although perfectly innocent, have the potential to be misinterpreted.

This research was inspired by a story reported in the national press. A young couple had moved house only 15 months after moving there to avoid young yobs who would pose outside their house, bare their buttocks and take photos – taxi drivers would not show up and takeaways would not deliver food because they thought the calls were hoaxes.

And all because the name of their street was Butt Hole Road.

Thinking that the name was rude, many people would crack terrible jokes at the couple's expense, saying things like, 'Is that near the ringroad, or the bottom of the street?'

As the local council had no record of why the street was so named, no-one could explain how the name was quite innocent; in all probability it originated as a reference to a nearby water source. We hope that the research presented here will mean that others who suffer from a similar problem will now have an authoritative explanation of their place and street names.

Once we set about researching this topic, we discovered an almost limitless number of potentially rude-sounding names. Some are land features, like The Devil's Beeftub, Lickham Bottom or The Bastard; some are woods or fields, like Cum Hag Wood; some are place names, like Lickfold, Nork or Lickey End; and others are streets such as Fanny Avenue, Willey Lane, Honey Knob Hill, Titty Ho or Asshouse Lane.

It is only natural that initially a reader may laugh at such unusual names, but we hope that, as their historical origins are explained, this tendency to titter will fade away. We hope to educate and illuminate by sharing the great learning we have experienced in compiling this book. If we are successful in our aims, we will have taken you, the reader, on a journey through our beautiful land and together have reclaimed the proud place names of Britain.

Rob Bailey and Ed Hurst

JEFFRIES PASSAGE

100

Guildford, Surrey Alleyway Map 5 D1

A Narrow Place

In the heart of historic Guildford, adjoining two of the main shopping streets, you will find Jeffries Passage. The narrow thoroughfare plays host to a variety of businesses from bars and shops, to an Internet café and an accountancy firm.

The name is of somewhat obscure origins, but probably refers to a family with local connections.

PRINCE ALBERT COURT 99

Sunbury, Surrey Street Map 5 inset

The Place
Prince Albert Court is a new, residential development branching off the A308 in Sunbury.

Princely History
Prince Albert (1819–1861), husband to Britain's Queen Victoria, has inspired the naming of many things, including pubs, streets and hotels. Victoria was grief-stricken after Albert's death; in testament to her love, a memorial designed by Sir George Scott was erected in Kensington Gardens in 1871 where there still proudly stands a monument to this man in the form of a huge golden Prince Albert.

NORK RISE 98

Banstead, Surrey Street Map 3 F4

From Rural to Urban...

Nork Rise is located in the suburb of Nork, close to the Surrey town of Banstead. The area has changed dramatically in character over the last century, from being largely rural and boasting an estate centred on the now demolished Nork House (built in 1740 for the Buckle Family), it has essentially become part of Greater London's suburban sprawl.

Etymology

The name is obscure in origin, but may derive from the phrase 'northern oak', presumably referring to a long-lost local feature. The modern, slang usage of the word 'nork', means 'breasts'.

BROWN WILLY

97

Cornwall Land Feature Map 4 C3

Associated with Swallows

This well-known Cornish hill stands firm and proud over the surrounding moorland. Rather incongruously, its name links literally to the Old Cornish for 'swallow breast' – deriving from the words *bronn* (meaning 'breast' or 'hill') and *gwennol* (meaning 'swallow', in the sense of the bird). This led to the name Brunwenely, which more colloquially means 'the hill of the swallows'. In turn, this has been corrupted over time to form the current name.

An Elusive Name

Despite its fame, this hill is surprisingly shy about its name. After spending a considerable time travelling long distances in the vicinity, the authors were unable to locate any sign mentioning the name.

GREAT TOSSON

96

Tosson Through the Ages

Situated close to Rothbury and the River Coquet, Great Tosson gives the impression of not having changed over the centuries. However, this rural community, now merely a few farm buildings and houses, was once a flourishing hamlet with blacksmiths, joiners' shops, a public house and a school.

Tosson Tower

Perhaps the best-known historical feature of the area is Tosson Tower, built as part of a system of defences against the Scots. The interested reader is directed to the excellent webpage entitled 'Things to do at Tosson Tower'.

Etymology

The name evolved from the Old English words *tot* (meaning 'lookout') and *stan* (meaning 'stone'). Thus the name means 'the greater place by the look-out stone', differentiating it from the nearby village of Little Tosson. This nearby hill provided inspiration for the Northumbrian pipe tune 'On Tosson Fell'.

TRUMP STREET

95

London Street Map 5 inset

A Musical Past

Not far from St. Paul's, and facing Prudent Passage, this street has a long and fascinating history. In modern times, the area is dominated by coffee shops and offices. However, centuries ago this was a place where 'trumpers' (makers of trumpets) were based.

Godly Trump

For a Biblical example of this usage of the word 'trump', see 1 Corinthians Chapter 15, 52:

'In a moment, in the twinkling of an eye, at the last trump: for the trumpet shall sound, and the dead shall be raised incorruptible, and we shall be changed.'

ST. MELLONS 94

Cardiff, South Glamorgan Village Map 3 C4

Sacred Origins

A church of this name stands in the village where St. Mellon was supposedly born into the noble Probus family. As a young man, St. Mellon left this district, on the outskirts of Cardiff, to adopt a much humbler life abroad.

He travelled to Rome before eventually becoming the Bishop of Rouen in France. He died at the age of 85, which would seem fitting as the village is also known as Old St. Mellons. He endured many self-imposed hardships, including a metal girdle that was said to be so tight-fitting that it cleaved his flesh.

Further Reading

Readers interested in the ecclesiastical history of Wales might wish to refer to a book by G. Davis, published in 1888 by Hodder & Stoughton, called *Flashes from the Welsh Pulpit*.

PERCY PASSAGE

93

Location

Situated close to Goodge Street in London, this little passageway is surrounded by offices, pubs and desirable dwellings.

From Gunpowder to the Moon...

The origins of the name are somewhat obscure, but may well be related to the Percy family. This illustrious family has been involved in some of the most important events in British history. For example, Henry Percy (the 9th Earl of Northumberland) became the patron of the first man to map the surface of the moon. He was also imprisoned for 15 years because his cousin, Thomas Percy, had been involved in the Gunpowder Plot of 1605.

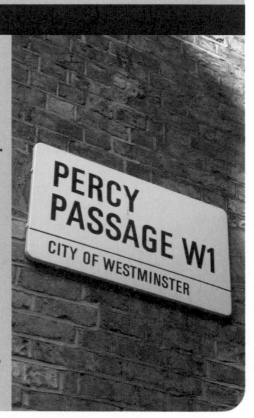

BOOTY LANE

92

Heck, North Yorkshire Street Map 2 G4

The Place

Booty Lane, tucked away in Great Heck, is a quiet track leading to a few houses and open fields.

Great Heck is a sprawling village hidden down twisting country lanes.

Footwear or Spoils of War?

The name 'Booty Lane' is of uncertain origin, but may indicate a history of boot-making in the vicinity. A viable alternative is that it is associated with the Booty family, whose origins lie in East Anglia. The surname may also be related to a history of boot making, or alternatively to the spoils ('booty') obtained from the Viking conquest of the eastern part of Britain.

NETHER WALLOP 91

Hampshire Village Map 5 B1

Three Wallops

Strung out along the banks of a Hampshire stream known as Wallop Brook, are three villages known collectively as 'The Wallops': Over Wallop, Middle Wallop and Nether Wallop. The villages are characteristic of the area – homely, charming and timelessly peaceful.

The attractive church in the village was used in the much-loved BBC adaptations of Agatha Christie's 'Miss Marple' stories.

A Spring in a Valley

The name Nether Wallop, which evolved from the earlier form Netherwellop, is probably based on the Old English words *wella* or *wælla* (meaning 'spring' or 'stream') and *hop* (meaning 'remote valley'). Thus it means 'lower place in a valley with a spring'.

Alternative theories suggest that the name may be based on the word *walu* (meaning 'ridge' or 'embankment') or *weall* (meaning 'wall').

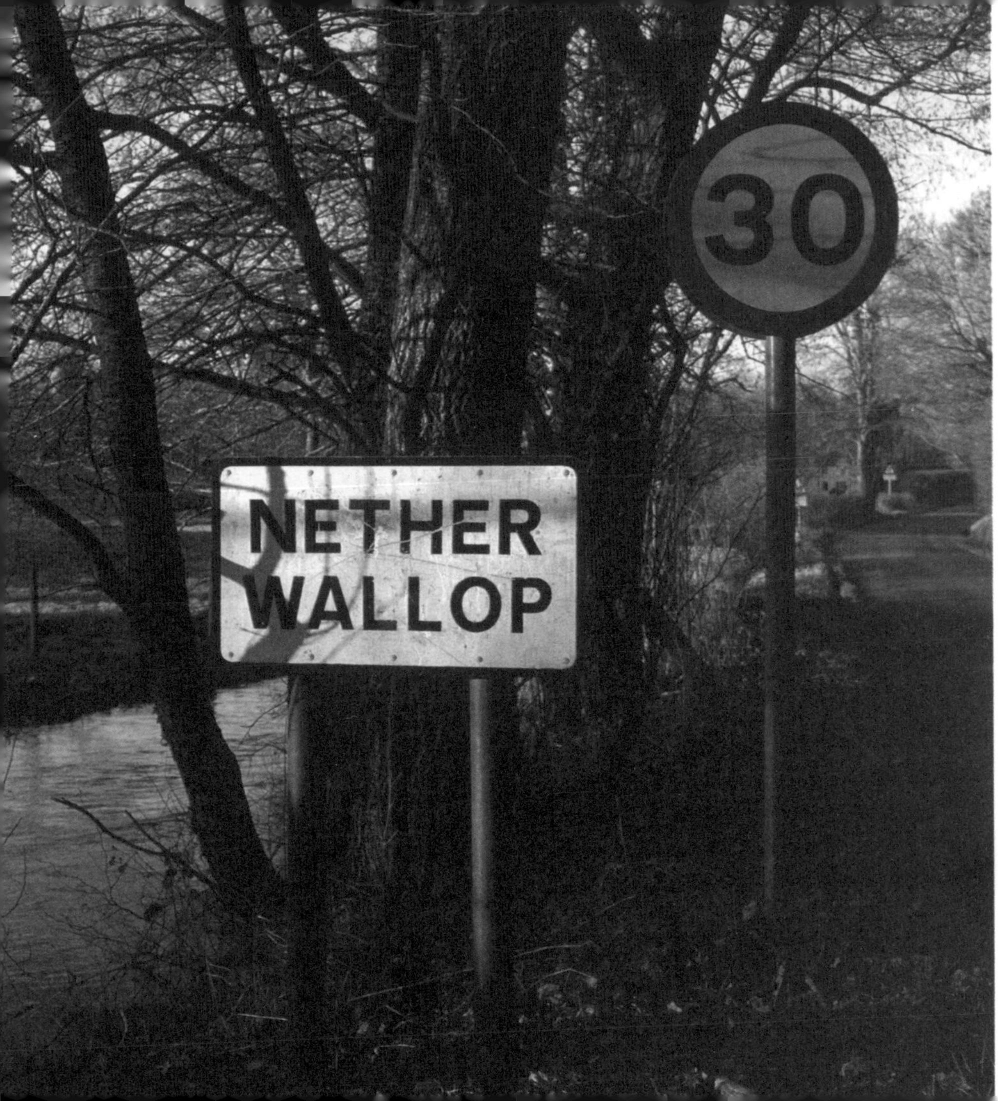
30
NETHER
WALLOP

HONEYPOT LANE 90

A Timeless Place

Situated in Husbands Bosworth in Leicestershire, this road has a timeless quality, providing a haven of peace close to a major thoroughfare. In common with much of the village, red brick and slate predominate, some of the buildings dating back to the 18th century. Close by is Honeypot Farm, the last remaining farm in the village.

Etymology

The name is probably an allusion to the area's rich farmland, honey being traditionally thought of as epitomising the bounties of nature.

MUDCHUTE

89

London Suburb / Land Feature Map 5 inset

Many people will only have become aware of this East London name when a station was opened here on the Docklands Light Railway in the 1980s. It refers to an area of open land created over 150 years ago as a by-product of the building of Millwall Dock. When this was developed, a considerable quantity of spoil was generated, which was simply dumped on nearby land. Silt that accumulated in the dock was then dumped on top of the spoil. This formed the place known as 'The Mudchute', which has become an open green space in an otherwise urban area. The surrounding area is now also referred to by this name.

JUGGS CLOSE

88

A Town of Juggs

Sitting in a charming hollow, within view of the rolling curves of the South Downs, is the East Sussex county town of Lewes. It is here that you will find Juggs Close (also Juggs Road and Juggs Lane), and the nearby pub called 'The Juggs'.

Fishy Origins

Only a short distance away from Pipe Passage and Rotten Row, Juggs Close is steeped in the history of the area. 'Juggs' (with two 'g's) were the baskets in which fish were carried, evoking the days when fishermen used to convey their catch from Brighton to Lewes. Similarly, 'Jugs' (with only one 'g') were Brighton fishermen – a linguistic similarity which must have led to some confusion.

COCKERMOUTH GREEN 87

Newcastle upon Tyne, Tyne & Wear Row of Houses Map 2 G2

Still a Community
This row of houses is situated in East Denton, a suburb of Newcastle upon Tyne. It is set back from main roads and has a community feel, largely because it overlooks a park much used by local children.

From Lakeland to the Tyne
Cockermouth Green is named after a famous Lakeland town. It is situated at the confluence of the Rivers Cocker and Derwent, and is a favourite site of lovers of the poet Wordsworth, who lived there for a number of years. Its name refers to the mouth of the River Cocker. *Cocker* is a common Celtic name for a watercourse, literally meaning 'crooked'.

SIX MILE BOTTOM 86

Cambridgeshire Village Map 3 E3

The name of this place is self-explanatory, situated as it is at the bottom of a valley 6 miles away from Newmarket.

It has suffered the fate of so many rural communities – its post office closed some years ago, and it has no school of its own. Happily, the public house still survives, providing one remaining focal point for the locals.

COCK AND BELL LANE

85

Long Melford, Suffolk Street Map 3 G3

An Ancient Pub

In the high street (known as Hall Street) of picturesque Long Melford, stands the 300-year-old 'Cock and Bell' public house. The bright pub sign shows a multicoloured cockerel examining a nest of two eggs, neatly arranged inside a shiny golden bell. The cockerel seems to be surprised by the clapper of the bell, which looks suspiciously like a third egg.

A Lane with a Rear Admiral

Cock and Bell Lane is likely to have derived its name from the pub. The sign for Cock and Bell Lane can be found on the side of a building once inhabited by Rear Admiral William Hanwell. He died at this house in June 1830, aged 64.

LITTLE BUSHEY LANE

84

Bushey, Hertfordshire Street Map 3 F4

Little but Long
Little Bushey Lane is on the outskirts of Bushey, in the northern extremity of Greater London.

Ironically, given its name, this is a long road which extends for approximately two miles through the northerly parts of Bushey.

An Enclosure
The name 'Bushey' comes from Old English, and means 'enclosure near a thicket, or hedged with box-trees.'

TITLINGTON MOUNT 83

Northumberland Hamlet / Land Feature Map2 G1

A Hamlet amongst Hills...

Situated in a peaceful part of Northumberland, Titlington Mount is both a hill and a hamlet, set amongst rolling hills and green fields, close to a village called Titlington. A nearby stream is called Titlington Burn.

Etymology

The name derives from the Old English *ing*, meaning 'associated with' and *tun*, meaning 'estate' or 'farmstead'; thus the name means 'estate associated with Titel', probably referring to a person who once owned land in the area.

SLIPPERY LANE 82

Faded Glory

Slippery Lane, located in the Hanley area of Stoke-on-Trent, presents a derelict and desolate scene. It was once completely surrounded by industrial buildings; prominent amongst these were the pottery works of Alcock, Lindley and Bloore Ltd. who made 'Brown Betty' teapots. After years of disuse, many of these buildings have been pulled down but have not been replaced. An abandoned sports ground nearby adds to the atmosphere of faded glory.

A Slippery Slope?

The origins of the name are not entirely clear, but may simply refer to the fact that the street is inclined, making it potentially slippery. Another plausible explanation is that the lane used to provide a convenient shortcut between the factories, allowing people to 'slip' easily through the area.

HOOKER ROAD

81

Hooker Road can be found in the tightly packed residential streets of east Norwich.

Hooker Road was named after William Jackson Hooker, born in central Norwich on 6th July 1785. He had a distinguished career as a botanist which took him on foreign expeditions, to the Chair of Botany at Glasgow University and culminated in his becoming the Director of the Royal Gardens at Kew, before he died, aged 81, in London.

CUMLODEN COURT

Newton Stewart, Dumfries & Galloway Street Map 2 D2

Hidden History

Cumloden Court is a residential road, situated in the hamlet of Cumloden on the outskirts of Newton Stewart. This is a quiet part of Dumfries & Galloway, overlooking an inlet of the Solway Firth.

The place is steeped in the history of Scotland. It is said that Robert the Bruce sought help here when on the run from the English, and secured the help of the three sons of a local widow. Such was their success at the Battle of Glentrool that the family was rewarded by being given the lands around Cumloden. The family lived at Old Risk Castle, and the ruins are still visible.

A Wet Place

The name may be related to the Gaelic words *cum* (meaning 'keep' or 'retain') and *lodan* (meaning 'little pool'). According to this explanation, the name means 'the pool that retains water'.

TINKERBUSH LANE

79

Wantage, Oxfordshire Street **Map 3 E4**

This is a short residential street in the suburbs of Wantage, a historical market town in Oxfordshire.

Tinker can mean an itinerant mender of household utensils or has been used to describe gypsies (often in a derogatory way). Thus it's possible that this street name refers to a long-gone clearing in a wood where gypsies lived.

UGLEY 78

Essex Village **Map 3 E3**

An Active Social Scene

Close to Stanstead Airport, this well-kept village is rich in clubs and societies for its residents. These include the Ugley Keep Fit Class, Ugley Friendship Club (Over 60s), and the Ugley Women's Institute. A rumour is often mooted that the Women's Institute has renamed itself 'The Women's Institute (Ugley Branch)'.

Ugga's Wood

The pronunciation of the name is commonly held to be 'usley'. Its derivation is thought to have come from the Old English word *leah*, meaning 'wood', and a local person named Ugga, who lived in a wood clearing here. It is listed in the Domesday Book (1086) as Ugghelea.

PRATTS BOTTOM

77

Rolling Hills

Pratts Bottom can be reached by descending via a tree lined B-road from hills in north Kent. The hills in question form part of the same rolling landscape responsible for the name of the nearby Badgers Mount.

Pratts in the Meadows

The meaning of the name is 'the village at the bottom of a hill, where the Pratt family live'. They are said to have resided here since the 14th century. The name Pratt comes from the Latin word *pratum*, meaning 'meadow'; therefore originally it may have meant 'the dwellers of the meadow'.

RAMSBOTTOM LANE

76

Bury, Greater Manchester Street **Map 2 F4**

Ramsbottom Lane is a short stretch of the A676 leading to Ramsbottom from the north of Bury.

Its name is thought to have come from one of two Old English sources, meaning either 'the valley of the wild garlic' (*hramsa + bothm*) or 'the valley of the ram' (*ramm + bothm*).

PRICKWILLOW

Cambridgeshire Village **Map 3 G2**

A Murky Past

This village is only a short distance from Feltwell on the Norfolk edge of The Fens. The name Prickwillow comes from the swampy past of this area when willow and reeds grew in the peaty waters. The willow was collected to make 'prickets', which were wooden skewers to hold a thatch in place.

Draining Prickwillow

The Fens were drained over time, using a variety of wind, steam and oil technologies. Drainage enthusiasts maintain the Prickwillow Drainage Engine Museum, which holds a collection of restored oil-burning engines.

OLD SODBURY 74

From Soppa to Sodbury

Old Sodbury's name comes from the corrupted Old English, and originally would have meant 'the fortified village of Soppa'. The fortifications refer to a Roman fort established here. More recently, in Saxon times, the Domesday Book lists a settlement called Sopeberie, a name that eventually became Sodbury. The prefix 'Old' was added to distinguish the older settlement from nearby Chipping Sodbury, which grew in prominence from the 12th century as a market town.

A Place to Camp

The Romans are likely to have established camp here as the place was en route to several important places, namely *Aqua Sulis* (Bath), *Glevum* (Gloucester) and *Corinium* (Cirencester).

UPPER DICKER

73

East Sussex Village Map 5 F2

Come to Dicker for Shelter

Twelve miles from Eastbourne, Upper Dicker is a very attractive village whose history is bound up with the priory at Michelham. This was set up primarily as a shelter for people travelling between the two conurbations of Battle and Lewes.

A History of Barter?

There are two credible theories explaining the origins of the name. One relates to the village's history as a centre of local trade – with travellers 'dickering' (bartering) their wares with local tradesmen.

The other explanation is based on the belief that the village was originally built on a plot of land, for which 10 iron rods were paid as rent; this association with the number 10 led to the place being called Decker (from the Middle English word *dyker*, meaning 'ten' – related to the Latin word *decem*). This name in turn evolved to become 'Dicker'.

Upper Dicker is the highest lying of three associated places, the others being Lower Dicker and The Dicker.

SWELL

Somerset Village Map 4 G1

Between Two Currys

This Somerset village can be found on the A378 between the two curiously named settlements of Curry Rivel and Curry Mallet. Birdwatchers may be interested to know that there is a heronry situated here.

Etymology

It is possible that the name of the village comes from a well named after St. Catherine; the name 'St. Catherine's Well' may have become shortened and corrupted to become Swell. Ruth Tongue, an expert in folklore, claims that St. Catherine's was a wishing well, and adds, 'You must go round it three times at sunrise, but if it was crawled round counter-clockwise it brought an ill wish'.

BLADDA 71

Paisley, Renfrewshire Street Map 1 D4

A Watery Place

The Paisley street of Bladda is an unusual one in that it basically contains the Watermill Hotel and its car park. The hotel is built on the site of a watermill dating back to the 17th century. The street name does not feature in the address of the Watermill Hotel (instead the name of a larger adjoining road, Lonend, is used). Even the street's sign is understated because it looks like a wooden nameplate.

Links to the Bladda Fever Hospital

This area of Paisley was once home to the Bladda Fever Hospital. Either the street or the hospital is likely to have lent its name to the other; the origin of the word 'Bladda' is, however, obscure.

SNATCHUP 70

Redbourn, Hertfordshire Street Map 3 F3

An Obscure Name

Situated in Redbourn, Hertfordshire, Snatchup is a residential street tucked away from a nearby main road. The name is of obscure origin.

SPITAL·IN·
THE·STREET

SPITAL-IN-THE-STREET · 69

Lincolnshire Hamlet **Map 2 H4**

Roman Road

Spital-in-the-Street is a hamlet on the A15 in Lincolnshire. This section of the A15 traces the route of the Roman road known as Ermine Street, which linked Lincoln and York. The road dominates the few buildings that make up this place.

An Old Hospital

The name means 'hospital on the Roman road', deriving from the Middle English word *spitel* (meaning 'hospital') and the Old English word *strœt* (meaning 'Roman road', linked to the modern English word, street). Little is known about the hospital that once existed here.

SHINGAY CUM WENDY · 68

Buckinghamshire Village **Map 3 E3**

Surrounded by wide, open fields, Shingay cum Wendy is a quiet, rural collection of dwellings.

The word 'cum' means 'adjoined with', and is used when two places merge to become one settlement. Therefore at one point Shingay and Wendy ceased to be two separate entities and would have joined together.

PUMP ALLEY

67

By the Thames

If you travel along the High Street from Kew Bridge to Brentford, you will come across Pump Alley. Situated close to the River Thames, it clearly shows how the area has developed. While there are signs of significant industrial and maritime heritage, modern hotels and offices now mingle with period cottages.

An Old Pump

In recent times, this open street could hardly be described as an alley, indicating significant changes in the environs over the years. Given its watery location, it seems likely that the alley is named after an installation that pumped water into or out of the river.

OLD SODOM LANE

66

Dauntsey, Wiltshire Street Map 3 D4

Biblical Roots

A number of Sodoms can be found in the UK, with their names perhaps inspired by the city of the same name found in the Bible. Given the nature of that ancient settlement, it is somewhat surprising that it should spawn other place names. In the Bible, Sodom was destroyed by God with fire and brimstone due to the grievous sins of the inhabitants.

Insulting Origins

It is possible that some British place names had negative origins; unflattering or negative names may have been used by residents of neighbouring areas, which have gradually been accepted as part of the official name.

Old Sodom Lane leads to an area known as Sodom, near Dauntsey in Wiltshire.

LONG LOVER LANE 65

Halifax, West Yorkshire
Street Map 2 F4

Hilly Panorama
Situated on elevated ground, this lane benefits from panoramic views of Halifax and the bleak, hilly area that surrounds it.

Escaping Protection
It seems probable that the lane is a place where lovers went to walk and generally get to know one another, in an era when it was difficult to escape interfering chaperones. The word 'Long' is obviously an indication of the length of the lane itself.

This name is not to be confused with Long Lover Lane in Rimington, Lancashire.

EAST BREAST

64

Greenock, Inverclyde Street Map 1 D4

Greenock Docklands

The origin of this name is unclear. 'Breast' can be used as a noun to refer to the shape of a hill, or to the face of a mine or tunnel. The verb 'to breast' means 'to contend with or confront resolutely', which may indeed be true of the streets in this area of Greenock. The streets front the Firth of Clyde in this dockland area, and may have breasted many a storm.

The harbours here also include the areas of East India Breast and Dock Breast. They may simply refer to the watery boundaries of the docks.

DICKS MOUNT

63

Burgh St. Peter, Suffolk
Street Map 3 H2

Rural Suffolk

This road can be found in Burgh St. Peter, on the River Waveney, which is used for sailing and offers pleasant riverside walks.

A Richard of Old

Dicks Mount is a country road on raised land on the outskirts of the village. The name is likely to be an informal use of the name Richard, who may have been a former resident; therefore, the likely meaning is 'the hill where Richard lives'.

STAINES 62

Surrey Town Map 3 F4

Roman Origins

Staines has been a settlement on the Thames from Roman times. It is downriver from historic Runnymede, which was the location of the signing of the Magna Carta.

London's Limit

'Staines' comes from the Old English *stan* meaning 'stone'. It refers to a stone marking the most westward point of authority of London city during Roman times.

TWINNED WITH MELUN
FRANCE

STAINES

CRAPSTONE 61

Devon Village Map 4 D3

Heading north on the A386 from Plymouth, one can either drive into Dartmoor National Park or turn left by a large rugged boulder for Crapstone.

One website describes Crapstone thus: 'There doesn't seem to be much history in Crapstone, judging by the history books, the best of which seem to have forgotten that it exists.' Indeed, the origin of the name has been so hard to find, it appears that even history forgets why Crapstone is so called.

THREE COCKS

60

Gradual Development

Situated on the River Wye, Three Cocks is named after a local roadside hostelry that dates back to the pre-turnpike period. The development of the area was considerably encouraged by the appearance of the new road, a horse tramway and the railway. Initially the area consisted of ill-defined, small settlements, but over time 'infill development' helped to create coherent villages.

FELTWELL 59

Norfolk Village Map 3 G2

From Farms to Arms

On the edge of the Norfolk fens, Feltwell is a thriving agricultural village. It has an Anglo-American community due to the proximity of RAF Feltwell, used by USAF and Space Command.

Spring or Stream?

Two theories exist for the origin of the name: the first suggests that it comes from Old English meaning 'the place by the spring (well) where mullein (*felte*) grows' (see also Feltham Close). Mullein is a figwort plant characterized by its woolly leaves and spikes of yellow flowers. The second theory is that it means 'the settlement in the meadow by the stream'.

PANT 58

Shropshire Village Map 3 C2

Welsh Hollow

'Pant' comes from the Welsh, meaning 'hollow or valley'. Although this particular Pant is in Shropshire, England, many more can be found on the other side of the nearby Welsh border.

BALLS CROSS

West Sussex Village **Map 5 D1**

Close to Lickfold...

Balls Cross is a small West Sussex village, a little less than 2 miles from Petworth House and approximately 3 miles from Lickfold. The historic Petworth House boasts a park landscaped by 'Capability' Brown, and inspired paintings by Turner.

Etymology

Place names with 'cross' in them tend to have been so called due to Christian markings on the roadside or at the site of crossroads. In places like Charing Cross and Kings Cross, one would previously have found stone crosses, both of which marked crossroads and distances from other places.

Balls Cross is likely to have marked a significant road junction. Perhaps it was named after a family or a local inn called 'Balls'.

OGLE CLOSE

56

Ogle Close, in Prescot (Merseyside), is a quiet, residential street close to the A57.

A Link to the Trossachs?

One credible explanation of the name is that it was inspired by Glen Ogle in Scotland, a place well known to visitors to the Trossachs. It may also refer to the village of Ogle, 4 miles north of Newcastle, in Northumberland.

FRIARS ENTRY

55

Oxford, Oxfordshire
Passageway   Map 3 F3

Ancient and Modern

Friars Entry is a passageway in Oxford which connects the historic with the modern: at one end Gloucester Green can be found with its purpose-built flats, market and bus station, whilst, at the other, Magdalen Street's grand, stone buildings typify those of the surrounding area.

Holy Passage

A friar is a member of a religious order who combines monastic life with outside religious activity. Hence Friars Entry probably owes its name to the fact that holy men would pass through this passage, the link between their friary and the outside world.

NORTH PIDDLE

54

Worcestershire Flatlands

North Piddle can be found in rural Worcestershire. It is a quiet, flat location where the many peaceful, well-tended houses and gardens bask in relative isolation.

From Marsh to Stream

The Old English word *pidele* refers to a marsh or fen. Over time, the word evolved and lent its name to the nearby stream, Piddle Brook, and to the villages of North and Wyre Piddle. Both villages lie on the stream, but the 'North' and 'Wyre' prefixes prevent confusion between the two, and hint at the 4-mile distance seperating them.

Benefiting from the presence of water, lush, green fields surround North Piddle, where a number of different crops are grown.

MINCING LANE

53

London Street Map 5 inset

The Epitome of the City

This lane, home to Balls Brothers restaurant and Roman remains, is but a stone's throw from Queen Street. It is virtually a microcosm of the City of London – five days a week it is a hive of activity, housing the offices of insurance underwriters and commodity brokers, smart bars, a livery company and a Chinese restaurant.

The Lane of the Nuns

The name 'Mincing' is linked to the ancient words *mynechenu* and *minch*, meaning 'female monk' or 'nun'. This seems to be related to the nuns of St. Helen, who used to hold property in the area. Therefore, it means 'the lane of the nuns'.

BOTTOMS FOLD

52

Mossley, Lancashire Street Map 2 F4

Under a Steep Drop

This is a row of modern cottages in a small valley appropriately described as 'Bottoms Fold'. The street is nestled under a steep drop from the centre of Mossley (also known as Top Mossley); hence the street is at the bottom of a fold of land. However, it would be misleading to say that this is the direct derivation of the name. The lower part of Mossley is known both as Bottom Mossley and Bottoms. It is a fold in the area of Bottoms.

Several Arteries

Several arteries run through here: road traffic, a river, the Huddersfield Narrow Canal, and trains between Manchester and Huddersfield all flow a short distance from Bottoms Fold.

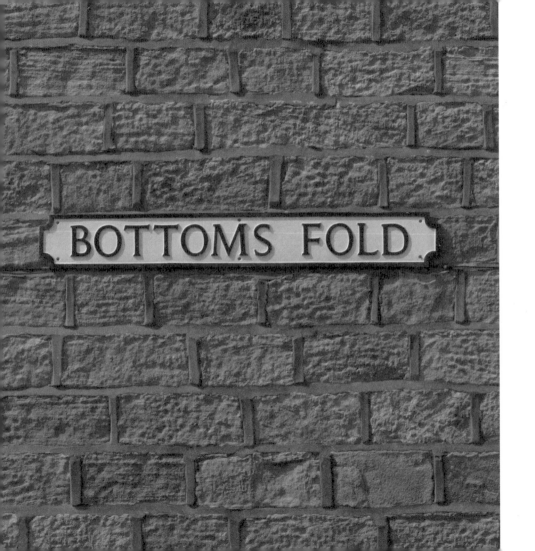

BACKSIDE LANE

51

Sibford Gower, Oxfordshire Street Map 3 D3

A Thriving Community

This is a peaceful country street in the Oxfordshire village of Sibford Gower. Seven miles from Banbury, and on the north-eastern fringe of the Cotswolds, the settlement boasts an active community with two pubs, two schools and two churches.

Simply a Backside

The origin of this name is clear: this street is around the back of the village.

WINKLE STREET

50

Down to the Water

Winkle Street in Southampton adjoins a historic section of the city's walls, and is close to the Museum of Archaeology.

Fishing for Periwinkles

There are several Winkle Streets in the UK (they are also to be found on the Isle of Wight and in Liverpool). Clearly they are all in areas associated with fishing. Winkle is short for periwinkle, a small marine snail, enjoyed by many as a seafood when cooked in boiling, salted water.

WHAM BOTTOM LANE

49

Healey, Lancashire Street Map 2 F4

Links to Swaledale's Peaks?
This is an easily missed lane branching off the A671 which leads to Healey from Broadley.

It might be thought that Wham Bottom Lane is named after Wham Bottom, one of the Swaledale Group of peaks in Yorkshire, standing at 2,171 feet. It is also possible that the lane is simply at the lower end of an area known locally as Wham.

A village called Wham can also be found in North Yorkshire.

UPPERTHONG

48

The Uppermost Area

Upperthong can be found poised on a hill in West Yorkshire. Reaching it via the steeply rising Upperthong Lane would challenge many a cyclist.

The name means 'the upper strip of land'. The neighbouring Netherthong is so named as it is lower down. Whilst upper and nether describe the location, thong means 'a narrow strip of land'.

Kirklees M.C.
Upperthong

TOSSIDE 47

Lancashire Village **Map 2 F3**

Amongst Rolling Hills

Situated on the border with North Yorkshire, this Lancashire village is full of the limestone buildings and dry stone walls so typical of the area. The country surrounding it consists of rolling hills and farmland, with Pennine views all around. Interested readers searching for the place on local maps should look just below an area marked 'Bent Ho'.

The name is of obscure origin, but may refer to the fact that the village is located on the side of a hill.

A small settlement nearby is called Tosside Fold.

THE FURRY

Helston, Cornwall Street Map 4 B4

The Furry Dance

Adjoining the shorter Furry Way, The Furry is situated in the Cornish town of Helston.

Helston is uniquely associated with a traditional Cornish folk dance known as 'The Furry Dance', which gave this street its name. The town still hosts an annual spring folk festival, in which children and adults alike do The Furry Dance in and out of buildings, along streets and up alleyways. The name is thought to derive from the Old Cornish word *fer*, meaning 'fair' or 'jubilee'.

LOWER SWELL

45

Gloucestershire Village Map 3 D3

Cotswold Spring

Lower Swell, near to Stow on the Wold and the Slaughters, is an historic village characterized by houses built of the local Cotswold stone. The discovery of a spring led to ambitious plans in the 19th century to develop the village as a spa, a scheme which met with little success.

Rising Ground

The name derives from the Old English word *swelle*, meaning 'rising ground' or 'hill'. Thus the name means 'lower place on rising ground', differentiating it from the nearby village of Upper Swell.

STOW-ON-THE-WOLD 1M

LOWER SWELL

CHELTENHAM 16M

LICKERS LANE

44

Situated in the Merseyside town of Whiston, Lickers Lane is a busy thoroughfare linking houses, shops, the community centre, a park and the local school.

The name probably originates from a member of the Licker family; the surname refers to someone who loves good food. The word is derived from the Middle Low German verb *licken*, which means 'to lick'.

HONEY KNOB HILL

43

Kington St. Michael, Wiltshire Street Map 3 D4

A Fruity Name

Situated in the Wiltshire village of Kington St. Michael, a small collection of cottages nestles here, slightly set back from the road. The name probably indicates that this was once a place in which pears grew and, in particular, a variety known as the 'Honey Knob'. This variety (not to be confused with the 'Clipper Dick', the 'Bloody Bastard' or the 'Startle Cock') was used to make perry, an alcoholic drink similar to cider.

No Link to Bee-Keeping

Some sources have speculated that this name has its origins in bee-keeping, or in the shape of the hill itself, but these explanations appear to be much less credible than the one described here.

BOGHEAD 42

Beith, Ayrshire Street Map 1 D4

Poor Drainage

There are many places called Boghead in the north of the UK, for example, and at least three can be found in Scotland: in Aberdeenshire, South Lanarkshire and East Ayrshire. The name is likely to be a reference to an area of poorly drained land.

This street comprises a collection of grand, stone houses and more modest bungalows.

A Wee Shame

A mere two-minute walk from Boghead is the site where a tiny passageway known as Wee Close used to be found; however, new building work has filled the space and deprived us of this quintessentially Scottish name.

THE BUSH 41

Haddenham, Buckinghamshire Street Map 3 F4

Home of a Duck

The Bush is a pleasant cul-de-sac of three houses in Haddenham, Buckinghamshire, which is the official home to the famous Aylesbury Duck.

Foliage & Wildlife

The name appears to be a simple tribute to leafy trees in the area. The three birds in the picture, although not obviously Aylesbury Ducks, appear quite at home in the foliage.

HILL O' MANY STANES 40

Scottish Stones

The origin of this site's name is obvious to those familiar with the Old English word *stane*, which in modern English is 'stone'. An alternative, but less poetic, name is the Mid Clyth Stone Rows.

An Astronomical Purpose?

On a gentle slope covered in gorse, approximately 200 stones can be found in neat north-to-south rows. Each one is from 1–3ft tall, and resembles a small gravestone even though no burials have been made here. They are thought to have been laid in approximately 1,900 BC, and may originally have numbered 250 in 22 rows, although some estimates are as high as 600. It has been suggested that the stones served an astronomical purpose, providing a reference for plotting the position of the moon, and enabling the community to chart the solar and lunar calendars.

On the 'End to End'

Due to its location just off the A9 south of Wick in the far north of mainland Scotland, this is a site that many 'End to Enders' pass by. These are travellers, including walkers, cyclists and vintage-car drivers, making the long journey from Land's End to John O'Groats at opposite ends of the UK.

GROPE LANE

39

Shrewsbury, Shropshire Street Map 3 C2

A Tight Fit

Situated in Shrewsbury, close by Gullet Passage and Dogpole, this steep, narrow lane is characterized by timber-framed buildings, evoking the atmosphere of old Shropshire. It is a very narrow thoroughfare, about the width of a large car. It is because of streets such as Grope Lane that some people have termed Shrewsbury 'England's finest Tudor town'.

A Shortened Name

The name Grope Lane derives from the fact that this was once the local red light district, though earlier forms of the name were somewhat more graphic. It was changed to reflect the sensibilities of modern times.

This is also a place that has inspired poetry:

Up Grope Lane,
Imagine a squeeze
or a hug
from a Bear on the Steps.
A low-beamed cafe
instead
'Mind your head'.

From 'A Day Out in Shrewsbury' by Meg Pybus

WILLEY 38

Willey is a small village bordering the A5, between Hinckley and Rugby.

Old English Wood

The source of this name is likely to be a corruption of the Old English words *wilig* (meaning 'willow') and *leah* (meaning 'wood'). Hence it means 'the place by the willow wood'. It is listed in the Domesday Book of 1086 as Wilei.

Other Willeys can be found in Devon and Shropshire, with a Willey Lodge in Herefordshire and a Willey Moor in Cheshire.

HAPPY BOTTOM 37

Corfe Mullen, Dorset
Hamlet / Street Map 5 A2

A Hidden Place

Happy Bottom is a small collection of dwellings butting onto the Dorset village of Corfe Mullen, near to the area known as East End. Although relatively close to a busy road, its seclusion is protected by the fact that reaching it involves travelling down a series of obscure but charming lanes.

The name appears to refer to the simple fact that it is a quiet and delightful spot, situated in a hollow.

FELTHAM CLOSE 36

Romsey, Hampshire Street Map 3 D2

Links to Greater London

Situated in Romsey, this street in a residential estate derives its name from the town of Feltham in Greater London.

Open Land?

There are differing views of the name's origins. Some say that it means 'the field village' or open land, whilst others argue that it means an enclosure in which mullein or a similar plant grows.

THE KNOB 35

Kings Sutton, Oxfordshire
Street Map 3 E3

This street backs onto a large recreational area in the remote village of Kings Sutton, Oxfordshire.

The word 'knob' is often used in place-naming to describe a rounded, isolated hill; however there is little evidence for such an origin here, as the surrounding area seems largely flat.

MENLOVE AVENUE

34

Liverpool Street Map 2 E4

Lennon Links

If you walk around the Liverpool suburb of Woolton, you will find Menlove Avenue. Only a short distance away from Penny Lane, this street is well known to fans of The Beatles, as John Lennon lived at No. 251 with his Aunt Mary until he was into his teens.

As a tribute to the years Lennon spent here, a posthumously released compilation of his work is called *Menlove Avenue*.

Alderman of Old

The street was named after Alderman Thomas Menlove (1840–1913), a draper and chairman of the local health committee.

TITTY HO

33

Raunds, Northamptonshire Street Map 3 F2

Moment of Fame
Situated in the village of Raunds, you will find Titty Ho. The village had a moment of fame in 2003 when it was visited by the Channel Four programme, *Time Team*.

Titty Family?
This street name is of obscure origin. The second word may be an abbreviation of the word 'house', perhaps indicating that a significant property was once situated here. The first word may suggest that it was named after local birds or a family with the surname Titty.

CROTCH CRESCENT

32

Oxford, Oxfordshire Street **Map 3 E4**

Crotch Crescent is a residential street, which can be found in the Marston area of Oxford, only a short walk from the famous John Radcliffe hospital.

A Lost Forest?

A 'crotch' is a fork in a tree. It is highly likely, therefore, that Crotch Crescent occupies the site of a bygone forest or orchard.

BLAIRMUCKHOLE & FORESTDYKE ROAD

North Lanarksire Street Map 1 E4 **31**

Pig Grazing?

This is an unremarkable road situated close to the M8 between Glasgow and Edinburgh. The source of Blairmuckhole is likely to be from the Gaelic words *blàr* meaning 'plain' and *muc* meaning 'pigs'. Therefore the area may previously have been a flat area of land used for the grazing of pigs.

Local Dykes

Forestdyke is most likely to refer to a ditch or watercourse running through a wooded area. A quick scan of a map will show that between this road and the village of Bonkle, another dyke-based name can be found: 'Dykehead'. Therefore dykes may have been a common feature of this landscape.

BLAIRMUCKHOLE AND FORESTDYKE ROAD

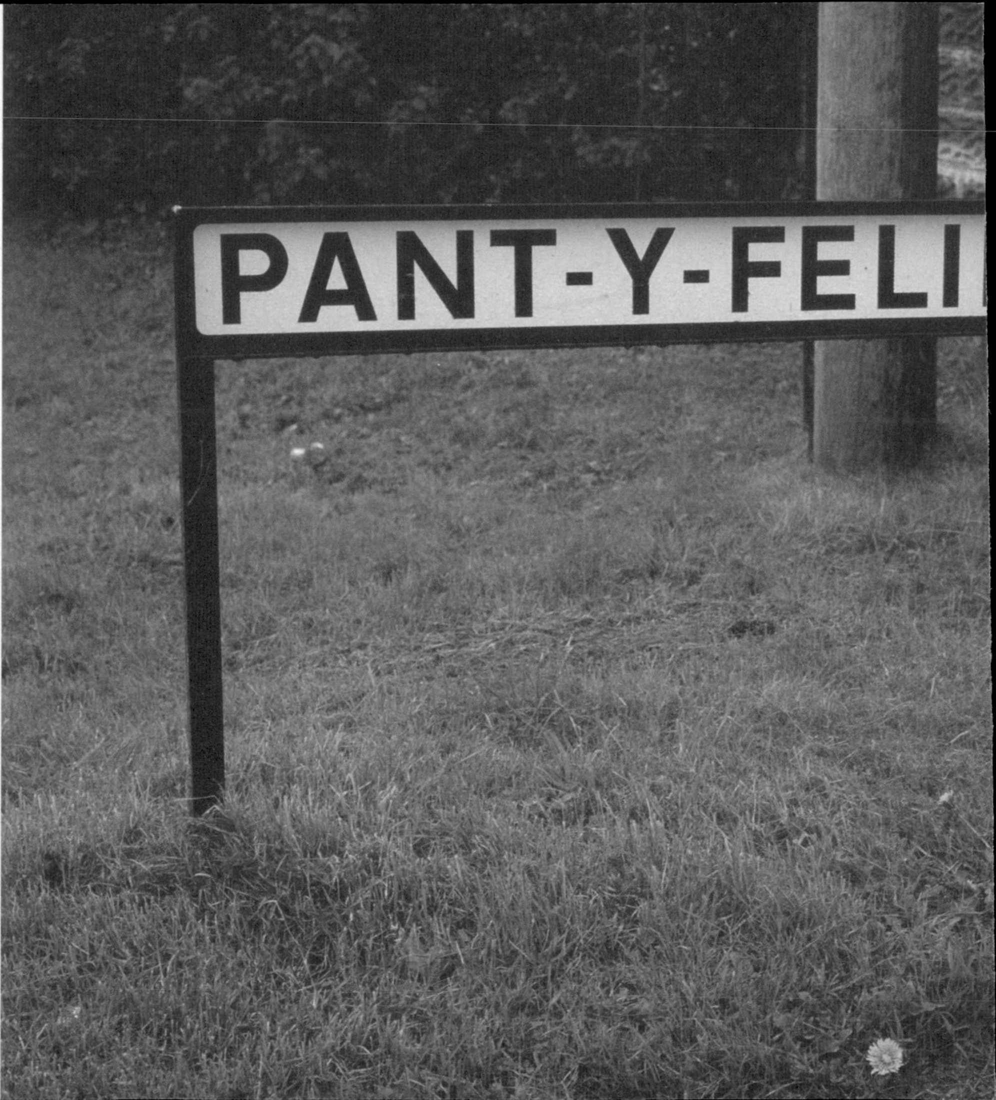
PANT-Y-FELI

PANT-Y-FELIN ROAD

30

Pontarddulais, Swansea
Street Map 3 B3

Urban to Rural

Situated in the village of Pontarddulais, west of Swansea, Pant-y-Felin Road begins as a fairly conventional street, consisting of houses and a driving school, but soon transforms itself into a rougher track serving some scattered cottages.

Welsh Origins

This Welsh name comprises a number of different elements. Pant simply refers to a hollow (or a valley), whilst y felin means 'mill' or 'the mill'. Thus 'Pant-y-Felin' loosely translates as 'valley of the mill'.

BEEF LANE

29

Oxford, Oxfordshire Street Map 3 E4

Frequented by Students

This street is owned outright by Pembroke College, part of the University of Oxford. It is opened on Sundays to the public to give access to a church. A term-time visit here is certain to find students busily going up and down Beef Lane.

Proud Butchers

As with many other historical places, this name is likely to have a professional origin. It is highly likely that in years gone by butchers would have proudly displayed their sausages and prime livestock products here.

MERKINS AVENUE

28

The Bonnie Clyde

Alongside the Firth of Clyde, is the town of Dumbarton. The A82, linking Glasgow with Fort William, runs through the area and close by is the Bellsmyre housing scheme, including Merkins Avenue.

Land Value

In mediaeval times, local lands were often named after the value of the rent that they could command. Land to the value of one merk (an old Scottish unit of currency) would be referred to as 'Merklands', or its diminutive form, 'Merkins'. Thus, Merkins Avenue was named after nearby land that was once worth one merk. This name in no way derives from the other meaning of the word merkin (a pubic wig).

PORK LANE 27

Pig Farming

A clue to the name of this road lies in the agricultural surroundings; the lane cuts through expansive fields and passes lonely farm buildings on its way to Great Holland in Essex. Pig farming is therefore the most likely source of the pork connection.

Keeping the Tradition Alive

A spirit of independent farming is still maintained in Pork Lane by a fruit farm producing cider, apples, pears and plums. The excellent farm shop also promotes locally grown food from other farms, for example fresh vegetables from Beaumont-cum-Moze, honey, jams and chutneys from Tendring, and meats from Wick Farm in Tolleshunt Major.

MOISTY LANE
26

Marchington, Staffordshire
Street Map 3 D2

Poor Drainage
This is a long, narrow and verdant country lane originating in the Staffordshire village of Marchington.

'Moisty' is merely another word for moist; hence the origin of the name may have come from the tendency of rural roads like this one to become waterlogged before the widespread use of tarmac.

Thick Undergrowth
The sign in the photograph was somewhat neglected and obscured, requiring a persistent trimming of the surrounding shrubbery to reveal it.

WETWANG
25

East Yorkshire Village Map 2 H3

Legal History
The name comes from the Old Scandinavian and means 'the field where legal trials take place'. In the original tongue, it would have been *wetuuangha* (the double u in the middle would be pronounced like our 'w' or 'v').

Readers may also like to note the explanation given in the book *'The Meaning of Liff'* by Douglas Adams and John Lloyd.

SCRATCHY BOTTOM

24

Dorset Land Feature Map 4 H2

Curious Contours

Walking along the rugged and steeply graded Dorset coastal path, you will reach Scratchy Bottom. It is thought that there was once a river here, and rain water still flows down the hillside and over the cliffs. Over the centuries, this process has taken a large scoop out of the chalk cliffs. The steep sides of this valley are in sharp contrast with the lush, grassy floor, providing an attractive and unusual scene.

Scratchy Bottom achieved unlikely exposure during the making of the well-known 1967 film, *Far from the Madding Crowd*, based on the Thomas Hardy novel. The curious scene in which Gabriel Oak's sheep plunge over a cliff was filmed here.

The name refers to the fact that the place is a rugged and rough hollow.

SWALLOW PASSAGE 23

London Passageway **Map 5 inset**

A Cut-Through

This tiny passage, close to Oxford Circus, is often used by office workers saving time on their journeys, for example when dashing to the nearby bank to make a quick deposit at lunchtime.

The origins of the name are obscure, but probably refer to a place where swallows nested many years ago.

LICKEY END 22

Worcestershire Village **Map 3 D3**

Lickey near Bromsgrove

Lickey End is so called as it is a settlement at the foot of Lickey Hill, close to Bromsgrove. The hill is one of those to be found in the Lickey Hills Country Park – a historic area spanning some 524 acres and including a raised point of land known as Lickey Ridge.

Rich History

Romans, royalty, J.R.R. Tolkien and many ramblers have been drawn to the hills. Those with a spiritual bent might wonder if this place exudes a strange mystical power (other than the force of Tolkien's magical ring). In his work *The Druidical Temples Of The County Of Wilts* the Reverend Edward Duke suggests that Lickey End is on an ancient lay line.

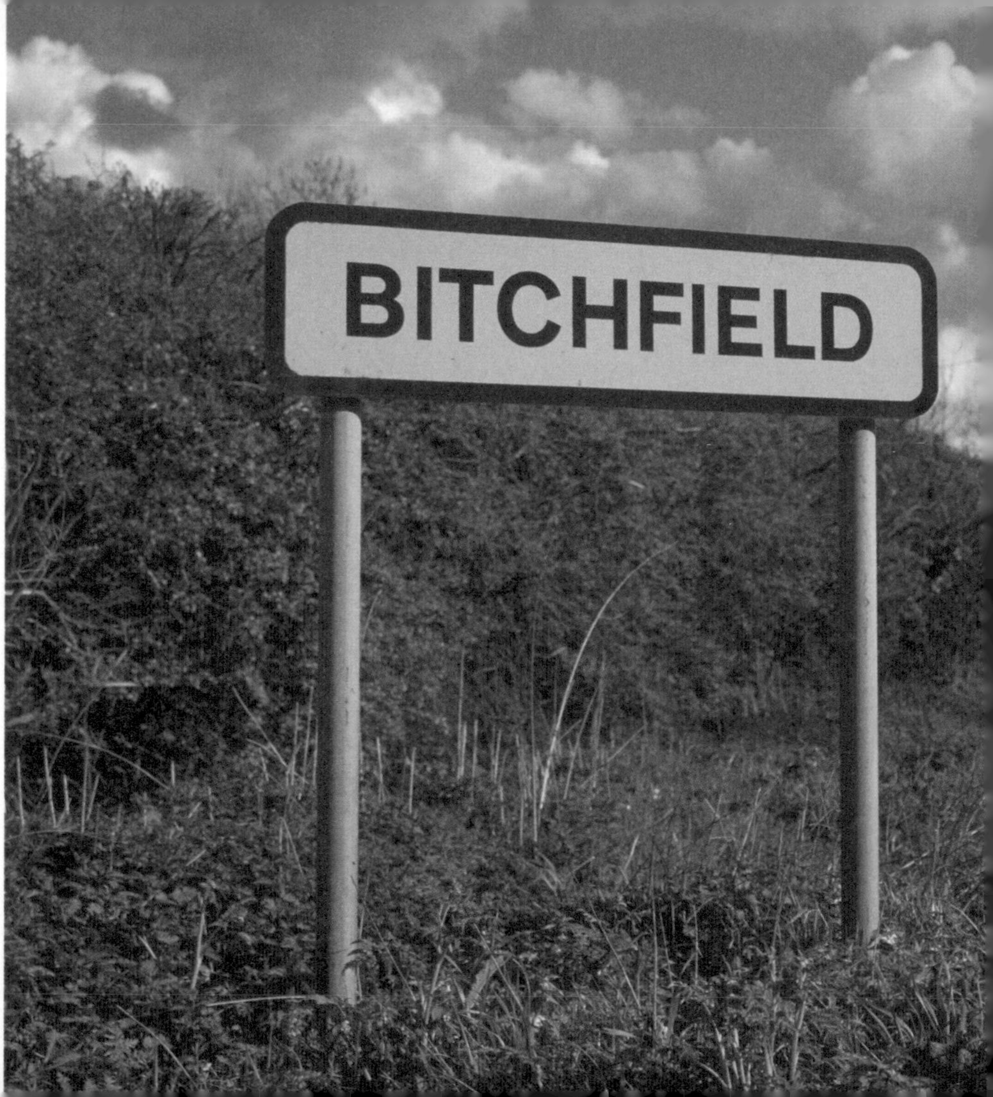
BITCHFIELD

BITCHFIELD 21

Bill's Field

Situated 7 miles from the market town of Grantham, Bitchfield is a village tucked away from the nearby A1 trunk road. Its name derives from the Old English Bill's *feld*, meaning simply 'Bill's field'. In 1086, the name was quoted in the Domesday Book as *Billesfelt*, later corruptions leading to the modern name. Nearby is the hamlet of Lower Bitchfield which should not be confused with the tiny Northumberland hamlet of the same name, situated close to Ogle and Saltwick.

SPANKER LANE 20

Nether Heage, Derbyshire
Street Map 3 E1

This has been named after the pub called The Spanker Inn, to which the lane leads.

Spankingly Good!

Chesterfield and District Campaign for Real Ale have done some investigation into the name of the pub, and believe that it was named after a 17th-century racehorse called Spanker, with form so impressive that it was once described as 'the best horse to run at Newmarket during the reign of Charles II'. Although somewhat old-fashioned now, the name seems to have come from the tendency to refer to items of quality as 'spankingly good'.

RIMSWELL

19

East Riding of Yorkshire Village Map 2 H4

A Spit near Hull

Rimswell, near Spurn Head in the East Riding of Yorkshire, is on the spit of land that juts out into the North Sea east of Hull. Perhaps its most prominent feature is St. Mary's church, modern by ecclesiastical standards, dating from 1800.

Etymology

The name 'Rimswell' is thought to refer to a spring or stream belonging to a man called Hrímr or Rými.

LICKFOLD

West Sussex Village Map 5 D1

This picturesque hamlet is situated in a quiet corner of West Sussex, approximately 5 miles away from Titty Hill.

Wild Garlic

The locality was probably given this name in the 13th century and it derives from the Anglo-Saxon phrase, *leac fauld*. *Fauld* refers to an enclosure in a forest clearing, created either for the growing of crops or the grazing of animals. *Leac* is less well understood, probably referring to the local wild garlic. Hence, Lickfold is probably 'the enclosure where the wild garlic grows'.

People of Lickfold

Lickfold also became a family name. The first recorded case of someone taking the name was the local Walto de Lykfold, who was probably born in the 13th century.

DICK COURT

17

Stonehouse, Lanarkshire
Street Map 1 D4

A Quiet Place

Dick Court is a cul-de-sac within a modern residential estate in Stonehouse, Lanarkshire.

It is likely that the streets in this estate honour people with local associations, giving rise to such names as Roger Court, Kane Place, McEwans Way and Brodie Place.

BEAVER CLOSE

16

Hampton, Surrey Street Map 5 inset

Urban yet Sylvan

The quiet backstreets of Hampton display an interesting mix of historic and modern architecture, each contributing to the atmosphere of the area. It is here that you will find Beaver Close. This cul-de-sac adjoins Hampton Football Club's ground. The nearby buildings are interspersed with shrubs and trees, lending the otherwise urban area a slightly sylvan charm, particularly when berries appear in abundance.

Links to Rodents?

Although the exact reasons for the name are not clear, it seems likely that it is simply an allusion to the aquatic rodent of the genus Castor, noted for its thick, brown fur, broad flat tail and sharp incisors.

FANNY AVENUE

15

Killamarsh, Derbyshire Street Map 2 G4

Fanny Avenue is situated in the small town of Killamarsh, between Sheffield and Worksop.

No Vegetation
This Derbyshire street embodies the archetypal close-knit neighbourhood of coffee mornings and twitching curtains. The word 'avenue' suggests a fairly important thoroughfare, lined on both sides with tall trees. In reality, this is a small cul-de-sac with head-high hedges.

A Local Lady?
The origins of this name are obscure. However, it seems likely that it relates to a famous lady called Fanny with local connections. 'Fanny' is a diminutive form of the name Frances, meaning 'free' or 'girl from France'.

COCKSHOOT CLOSE

14

Stonesfield, Oxfordshire Street Map 3 E3

Woodcocks
The origins of this name may come from bygone hunts for game birds called woodcocks.

Snaring Cocks?
Alternatively, the close might be named after Cockshutt, a village in Shropshire. This also owes its name to woodcocks, as the village occupied an area where people would attempt to catch the birds.

The usual method of snaring the birds was to put up a net to catch them.

A Norfolk Dyke?
Another possible, if less likely explanation, is the Cockshoot Broad, a long way away in Norfolk. This area is popular with boaters who like to glide up and down the Cockshoot Broad dyke.

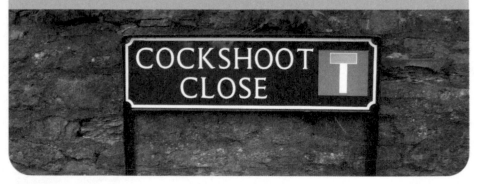

INCHINNAN DRIVE

13

Inchinnan, Renfrewshire Street **Map 1 D4**

Inchinnan Drive is located on the periphery of Glasgow Airport, and is named after the nearby village of the same name.

Gradual Growth

The earliest known settlement in Inchinnan dates back to 597AD. People entered the area only gradually, but in recent times have come much more rapidly. After a period of gradual growth, the development culminated in the building of factories and the airport.

Three Rivers or St. Mungo?

Since the word *inch* means 'an island' in Gaelic, some have argued that the name means 'Island of the Rivers', as Inchinnan is bound on three sides by the Rivers Clyde, Black Cart and Gryffe, whilst others have argued that the place took its name from St. Inan, a disciple of St. Mungo.

FANNY HANDS LANE 12

Ludford Parva, Lincolnshire
Street Map 3 F1

A Famous Fanny

This lane was once the home of a lady called Fanny Hands. Fanny was well-known in the area, frequently sitting at the end of the lane to watch the world go by whilst smoking her pipe. When she died (it is thought in the 1920s), it was decided to name the lane after her.

See also Fanny Avenue.

HOLE OF HORCUM 11

North Yorkshire Hamlet /
Land Feature Map 2 H3

Huge Hollow

In the heart of the North York Moors, this is a huge, natural hollow about 600ft deep and approximately a quarter of a mile across. A nearby hamlet has the same name.

Angry Giant or Simple Erosion?

According to local legend, the hollow was formed when a giant scooped up a great ball of earth to throw at his wife. Luckily, his toss went awry, landing close by to form the hill, Blakey Topping. In truth, it was formed by long-term erosion.

Only a short distance away is a plantation of trees known as Horcum Slack.

SLAG LANE

Haydock, Merseyside
Street Map 2 E4

Gone without Trace
Situated in the Merseyside town of Haydock, Slag Lane is a modern, residential street adjoining a small, wooded area. Recent building work has removed virtually all traces of industrial activity in the immediate vicinity.

The name simply refers to the slag heaps that were formerly so characteristic of the area.

SHITTERTON

Dorset Hamlet **Map 5 A2**

Important Outcomes...

Close to Yearling's Bottom, Shitterton is a hamlet adjoining the Dorset village of Bere Regis, a short distance away from Tolpuddle, a place made famous by the Tolpuddle Martyrs. In the 19th century, these six farm labourers set up a union to reverse their abject poverty, and their plight is often held to have played a major part in the formation of modern day Trade Unionism. Nearby Puddletown (formerly known as Piddletown) was the inspiration for the fictional town of 'Weatherbury' in Thomas Hardy's novels.

9

...with Prosaic Origins

It has been suggested that the name Shitterton simply means 'the village on the stream that is used as an open sewer'.

BACK PASSAGE

8

Tucked Away

Situated in the City of London, close to Smithfield Market and the Barbican, this obscure little alleyway is passed by thousands of people each week, yet most people remain unaware of its existence. It seems strange that so functional and secluded a place should have been named at all, but such idiosyncrasies are testament to the rich history of London.

A Simple Name

The name 'Back Passage' simply derives from the fact that it is a passageway running around the back of a row of buildings to allow access to their rear entrances.

CITY OF LONDON

BACK PASSAGE EC1

FINGRINGHOE

Essex Village Map 3 G3

7

Shaped Like a Finger

This lovely village can be found tucked away in a fold of land in Essex, below Colchester. The name means 'the place on a raised area of land (hoe), looking a little like a finger'.

Varied Pursuits

Towards the middle of the village can be found a military practice area (a small arms range), a post office, a green with a beautifully carved and painted village sign, and Fingringhoe Club. However, Fingringhoe is probably best known for the Nature Reserve at Fingringhoe Wick where a number of species of bird can be observed including Sand Martins, Turtle Doves and Nightingales.

MUFF

County Donegal, Ireland and County Londonderry, Northern Ireland Village Map 2 B1

Tribute to Ireland
Although the Irish town of Muff falls outside the scope of this British book, its inclusion is a tribute to the rich cultural history of Ireland.

A Plain Place
Situated primarily in County Donegal, this charming and neatly kept place can be found in both Northern Ireland and Eire, as it straddles the border. The name, which in its original Irish form is Magh, simply means 'plain' – referring to the area's simple appearance. To the east, the town is bounded by Lough Foyle.

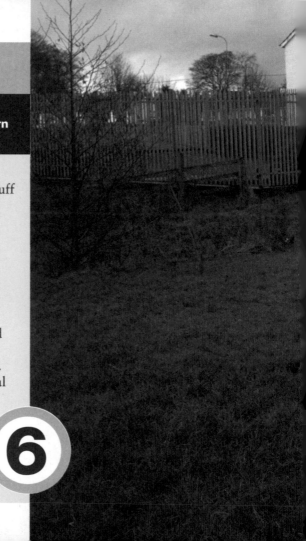

6

SANDY BALLS

Hampshire Place Map 5 B1

A Hunting Haven

Situated in the New Forest, Hampshire, this place is perhaps best known for its holiday centre. The Forest was originally designated by William the Conqueror in the 11th century for the purpose of game hunting, and it remains a haven of peace.

Dome-shaped Outcrops

The name 'Sandy Balls' derives from the lie of the land, namely dome-shaped gravel and sand outcrops that contrast so well with the local Scots pines. In the reign of Henry VII, it was known as Sandyballas, evolving first to Sandyballes and then to the current name.

Sandy Balls

TWATT

Orkney Village **Map 1 inset**

Shetland and Orkneys

If you travel north from mainland Scotland and visit the Shetland Isles or the Orkneys, you are likely to come across Twatt. Both island groups boast a place of this name, hinting at both their shared origins and their continuing separation.

Windswept

These islands are difficult to get to, but they certainly reward the effort. They combine a warm welcome with a beautiful, windswept solitude quite unlike anything offered even by the northerly mainland counties of Sutherland and Caithness.

A Clearing

Like so many place names on these islands, its origins are a mingling of Scots and Norse. It derives from the word *þveit*, meaning 'a parcel of land', or 'a clearing'. It occurs in quite a few Shetland farm names, such as Foratwatt, Brunatwatt, Germatwatt and Stennestwatt.

BELL EN

BELL END

3

Directly opposite Mincing Lane, Bell End can be found in Rowley Regis, a residential suburb on the outskirts of Birmingham.

Links to Bells?

The origins of this street name have been difficult to trace. Perhaps the street led to a church where musicians would ring their bells by hand or rope.

This Bell End is not to be confused with a hamlet of the same name less than 10 miles to the south. In a more rural location, and comprising only a handful of buildings, this second Bell End is a mere 5 miles from Lickey End.

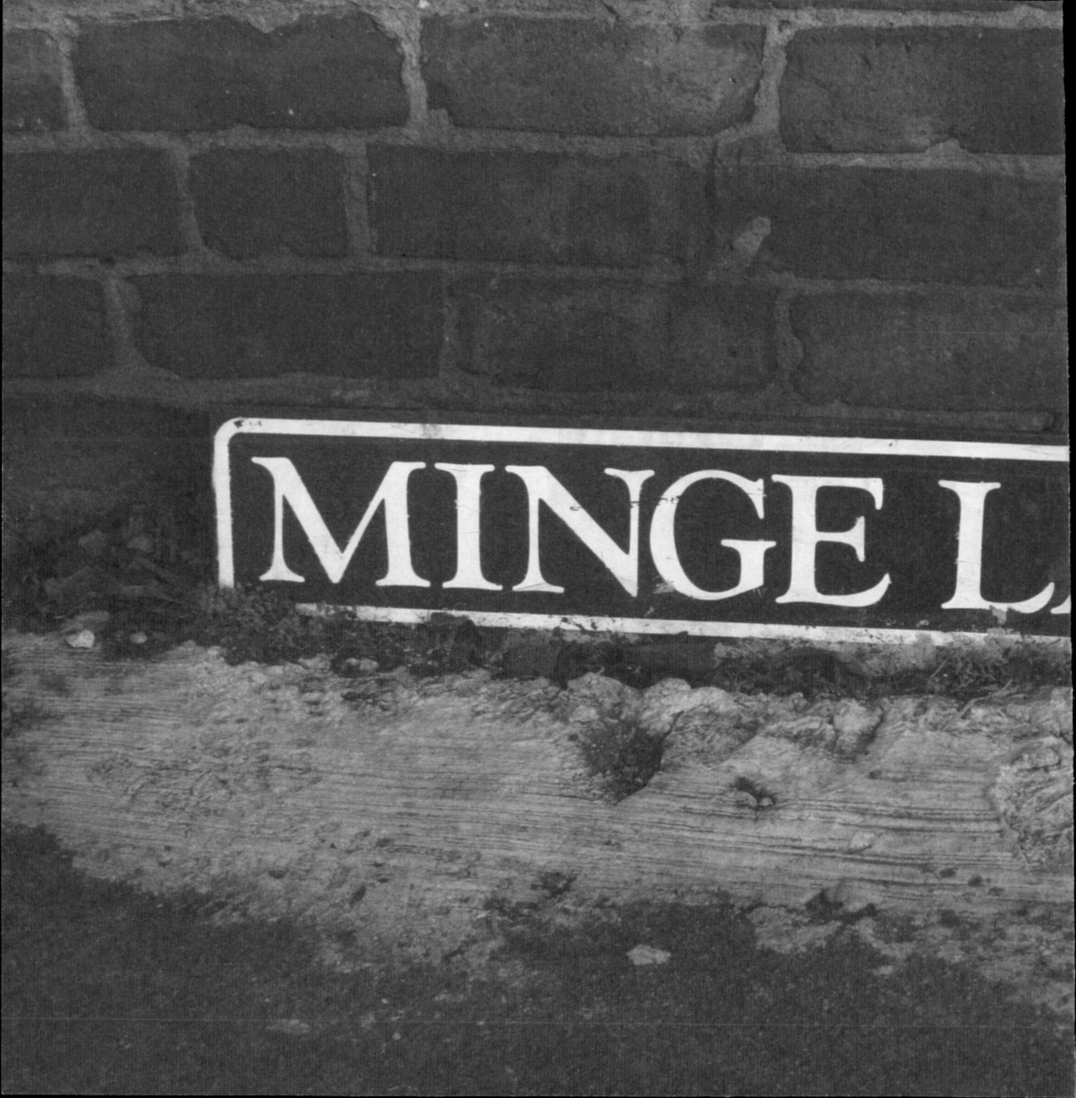
MINGE L

MINGE LANE

Upton Upon Severn, Worcestershire Street Map 3 D3

Mingling with Others

Situated in the pleasant Worcestershire village of Upton upon Severn, Minge Lane provides a reminder of the capacity of language to evolve. Although in its mother-tongue of English, the interpretation of 'minge' has developed over centuries, the American language preserves the original meaning of 'mingling with others'.

A fire station is situated here, at the junction of the larger A4104 road to Little Malvern. One or two appliances can regularly be seen parked in readiness for a call to action.

2

COCKS

Please drive carefully through the village

COCKS

Cornwall Village Map 4 B3

Popular for Riding

On a popular path for pony riders, in an undulating landscape, you will find Cocks. It is a small hamlet, consisting of little more than a few houses, close to the sandy beaches of Perranporth and Newquay on the North coast of Cornwall.

Connected with Birds

Typically, names including 'Cock' come from a connection with wild fowl or domestic birds. Cockerels and woodcocks are the most likely bet.

Puritanical Graffiti

Please note that alternative spellings for this place can be found (see below). Whilst this may appear to be an action of the council, the authors believe it to be nothing more than puritanical graffiti. However, you can see the true spelling in the photograph opposite.

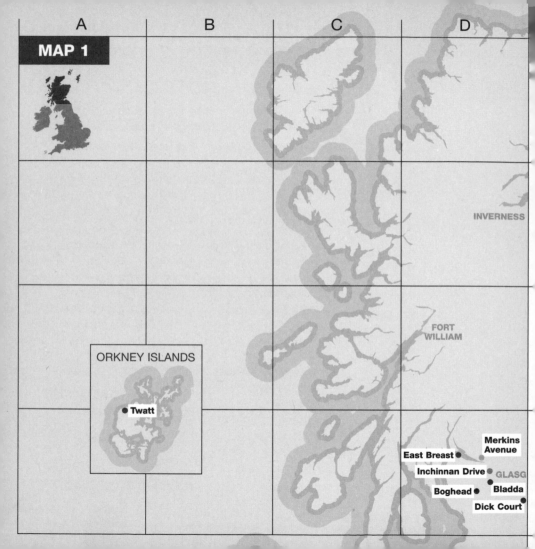

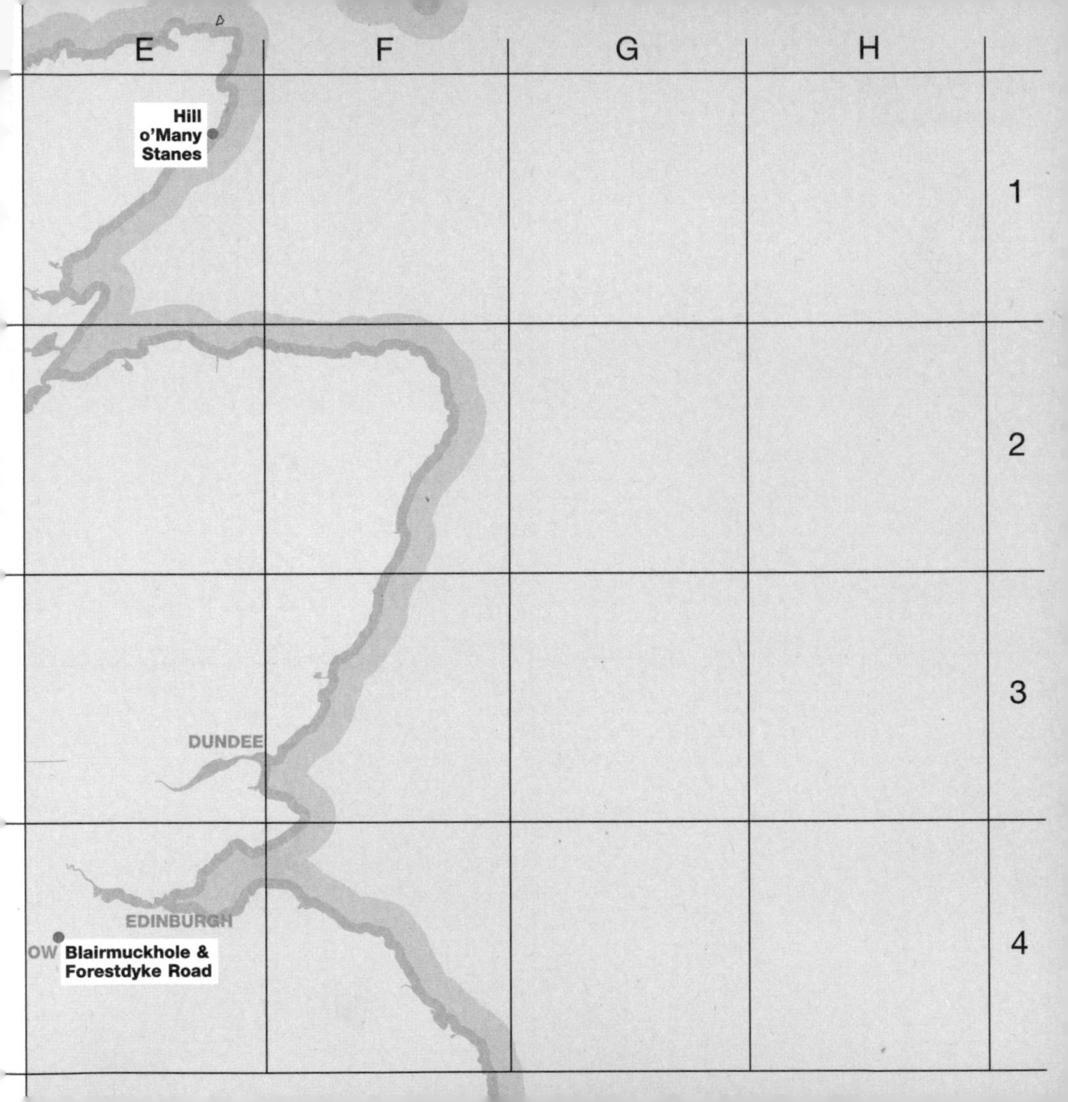
E
F
G
H
1
2
3
4
Hill o'Many Stanes
DUNDEE
EDINBURGH
Blairmuckhole & Forestdyke Road

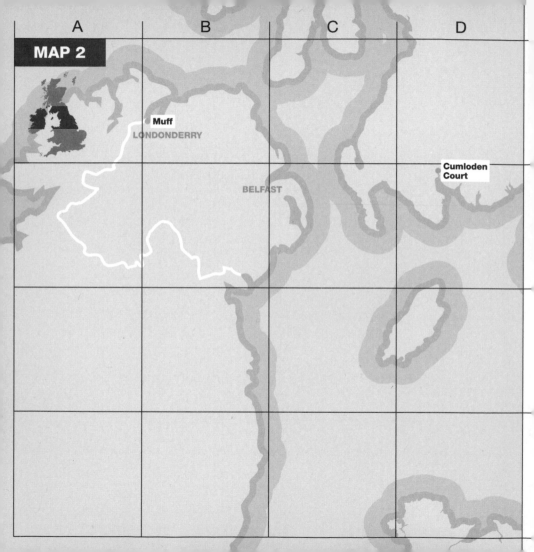

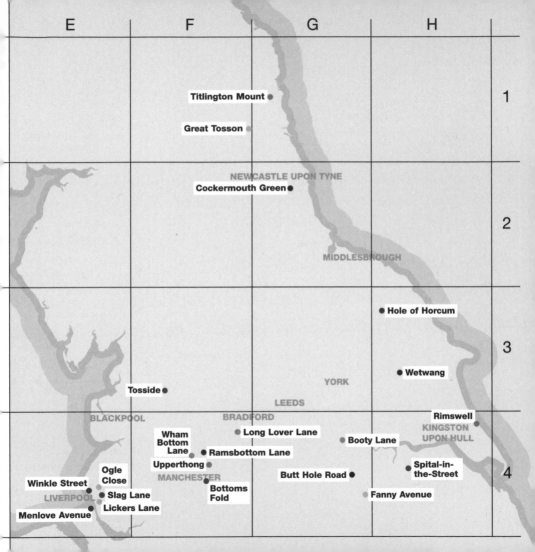

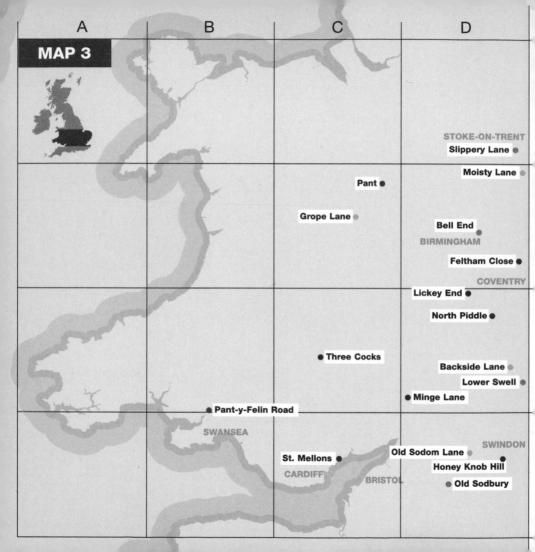

MAP 3

| | A | B | C | D |

STOKE-ON-TRENT
Slippery Lane ●

Moisty Lane ●

Pant ●

Grope Lane ●

Bell End ●
BIRMINGHAM

Feltham Close ●
COVENTRY

Lickey End ●

North Piddle ●

Three Cocks ●

Backside Lane ●

Lower Swell ●

Minge Lane ●

Pant-y-Felin Road ●

SWANSEA

SWINDON
Old Sodom Lane ●

St. Mellons ●

Honey Knob Hill

CARDIFF

BRISTOL

● Old Sodbury

	E	F	G	H	
1	● Spanker Lane NOTTINGHAM	● Fanny Hands Lane ● Bitchfield			1
2	● Honeypot Lane ● Willey	PETERBOROUGH ● Titty Ho	● Feltwell ● Prickwillow	● Hooker Road NORWICH ● Dicks Mount	2
3	CAMBRIDGE ● Six Mile Bottom Shingay cum Wendy ● The Knob ● Ugley ● Cockshoot Close ●	OXFORD ● Friars Entry	● Cock and Bell Lane IPSWICH ● Snatchup	● Pork Lane ● Fingringhoe	3
4	Beef Lane ● ● Crotch Crescent ● The Bush Tinkerbush Lane ●	● Little Bushey Lane ● Staines ● Nork Rise	LONDON (see Map 5) ● Pratts Bottom		4

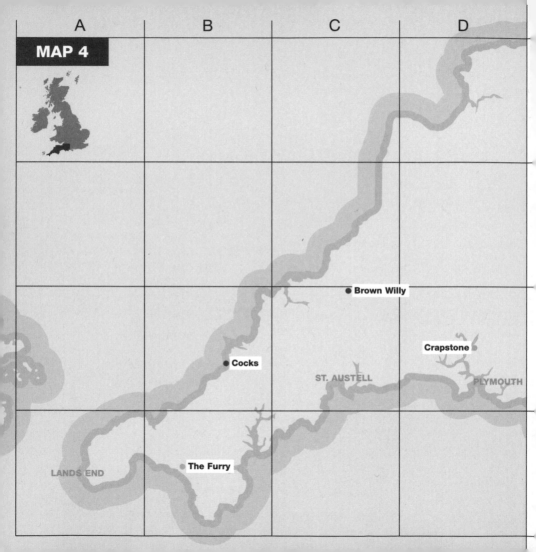

E
F
G
H
1
2
3
4
Swell
EXETER
DORCHESTER
Scratchy Bottom
TORQUAY

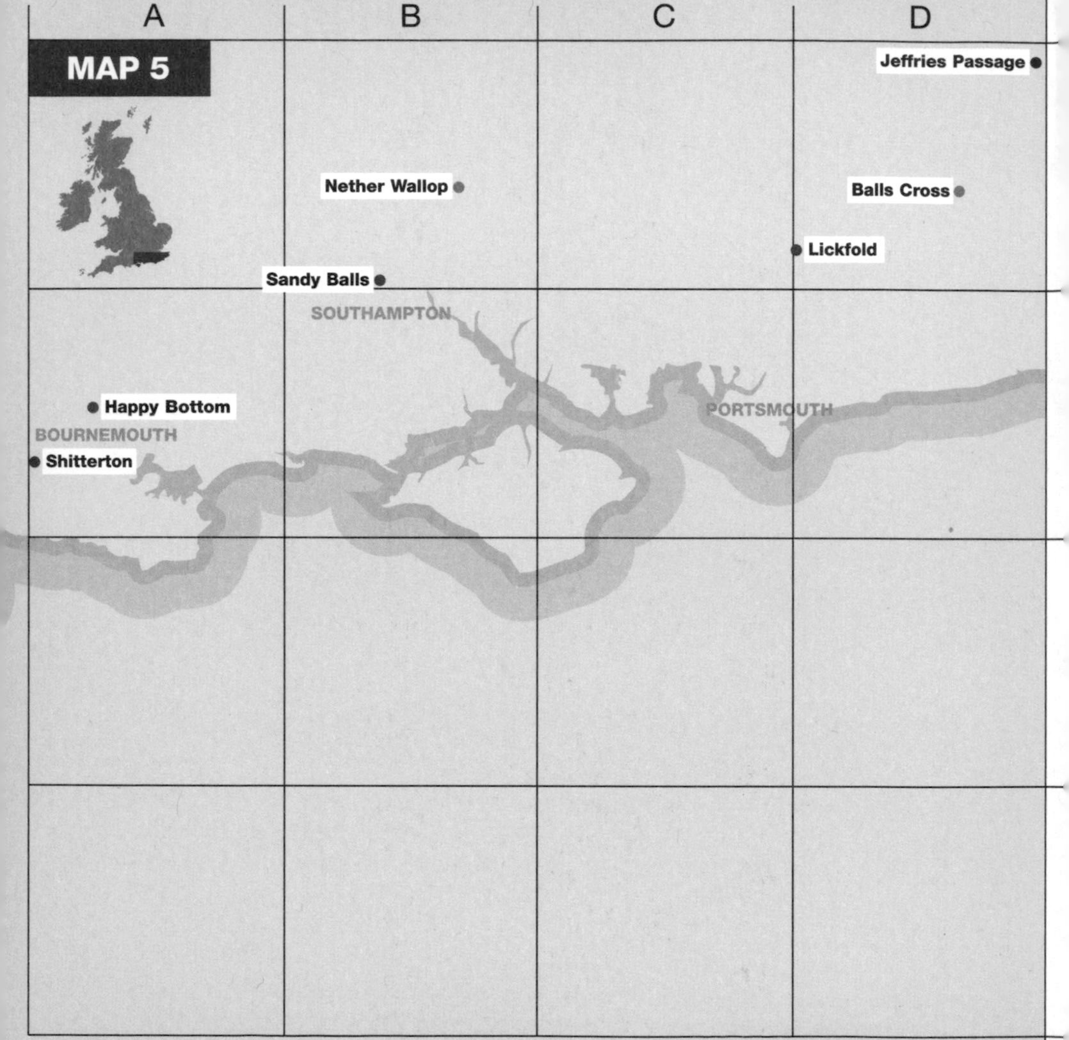

	A	B	C	D

MAP 5

Jeffries Passage ●

Nether Wallop ●

Balls Cross ●

● Lickfold

Sandy Balls ●

SOUTHAMPTON

● Happy Bottom

BOURNEMOUTH

PORTSMOUTH

● Shitterton

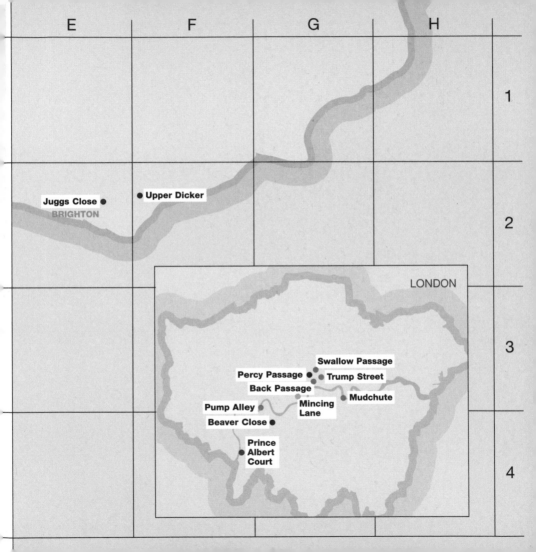

	E	F	G	H
1				
2	Juggs Close ● BRIGHTON	● Upper Dicker		
3			LONDON Swallow Passage Percy Passage ● ● Trump Street Back Passage Pump Alley ● Mincing Lane ● Mudchute Beaver Close ●	
4			Prince Albert Court ●	

SELECTED BIBLIOGRAPHY

The following works provide an excellent starting point for the study of the names of places, streets and people:

Mills, A.D., Oxford Dictionary of British Place Names (Oxford University Press, 2003).

Mills, A.D., Oxford Dictionary of London Place Names (Oxford University Press, 2001).

Room, A., The Street Names of England (Paul Watkins, 1992).

Spence, H., 7000 Baby Names, Classic and Modern (Foulsham, 2001).

Wallace, C.M., 20,001 Names for Baby (Avon Books, 1992).

Wittich, J., Discovering London Street Names (Shire Publications, 2003).

INDEX